Dottie & Diego
A True Love Story

R|W

C|W

First Publishing

Dottie & Diego
A True Love Story

ISBN 978-0-9827825-6-9

Copyright © 2011 by Connie Wilkett Weatherford

Published by
Goldfinch Oracles, LLC
113 N. 1st Street
McAlester, OK 74501

If you would like to purchase a copy of this book, please email the publisher at
gwenniepoo@sbcglobal.net

The Publisher's aim is to produce books for the edification and building up of the Kingdom of God. The Publisher does not necessarily agree with every view expressed by the author or interpretation of the scriptures. It is left to the reader to make his/her judgment in the light of their understanding of God's Word by the spirit.

Unless otherwise noted, all scripture quotations are from the King James Version of the Bible.

Printed in the United States of America

All rights reserved under International Copyright Law. Contents and/or cover may not be reproduced in whole or in part in any form without the express written consent of the Publisher.

Cover design by Gwen Titsworth. Illustrations by Cindy Barr and Gwen Titsworth
Goldfinch Oracles, LLC

This book is dedicated to my late husband, Ronnie, who had the faith that I could do just about anything.

A True Love Story

Tomorrow was the big day. Although I dreaded to see it come, I knew it was necessary. It had been eight weeks since my puppies were born, and eight means new beginning. My sweet little puppies would start on their own journey of life. I knew they would be given

choices so I wanted to prepare them for whatever was ahead.

I knew that what I told them today would leave a lasting impression. I did not want to leave anything out.

Sons and daughters gather 'round quickly, Mother has a story to tell you. Hurriedly the puppies gathered around me. They love it when I tell them stories.

Today, pups, I'm going to tell you a story about my life. I hope that you will always remember it; and, if you ever need me, the story will be a reminder of what to do.

My real name is Dottie Mae. I am an English Bulldog and I was born September 21, 2007. My human parents are Ronnie and Connie. My Mom, Connie, wanted me because her husband, Ronnie, was very sick.

She knew that I could give extra love to their family and that would make him feel better. Connie and Ronnie were Christians so they gave me a Christian name. Dottie means *a gift from God*.

Today, I want to share with you how I met your father. Just as I was waking up one morning, Mom came out to my little house. She seemed very excited!

She said, "Dottie, today is the first day of Spring. See how the flowers are blooming?! Oh my, and smell the air! That is the smell of love."

I knew something was different about that day; but, I didn't really feel that good. I have to admit it though, it was a beautiful day.

"Oh Dottie," said Mom, as she squeezed my cheeks and gave me a kiss, "how would you like to have a bull-friend? Your father and I met this wonderful Christian lady who raises English Bulldogs.

Your father has picked one that he would like for you to meet. Somehow, I knew that they had already made the choice for me; but, I had complete faith in them.

I waited eagerly to meet my new bullfriend. Several days had past. Then, early one morning Mom came and said, "Dottie, today is a special day. Today is *Easter Sunday;* and, this is the day that you're to meet your new bullfriend. Excitement filled the air!

As I started to the car, I suddenly felt scared. What if my new friend doesn't like me?! What if I don't like him! Mom could sense how I felt. She said with her soothing, gentle voice, "Don't be scared. I've prayed and everything will be alright."

    I knew how much she loved me; and if she liked him for me, he must be special. Mom drove me to my veterinarian, Dr. Phil. I was to meet my new friend at Dr. Phil's clinic. As Mom drove, she told me a little about my new bullfriend. She said his name was Gorgeous Diego and his human parents were Chuck and Jackie.

When we arrived we were greeted by our new friends. Everything Mom told me about them was true. It was love at first sight for both of us. My heart pounded with joy when Diego came to court. He was kind and gentle in nature. Diego displayed the virtues of meekness and temperance.

All too soon it was time to leave. As we left, I thought how much I loved my new friends and hoped to see them again. On our drive back home, Mom told me that she asked God to bless our union and give us a double portion. Little did I know what that would mean!

Days went by, weeks, months, and then the big day came – June 2, 2010. It was the day for me to go back to see Dr. Phil. It was the day you were to be born. Mom went in with me and I could hear her saying to Dr. Phil, "How many? Nine! Did I hear you say nine?!"

"Yes, nine!" exclaimed Dr. Phil. We were so surprised! Nine puppies for an English Bulldog is very unusual.

Now you can understand why Mom got so excited! 'Oh my,' I thought, 'I see what she meant by a double portion!'

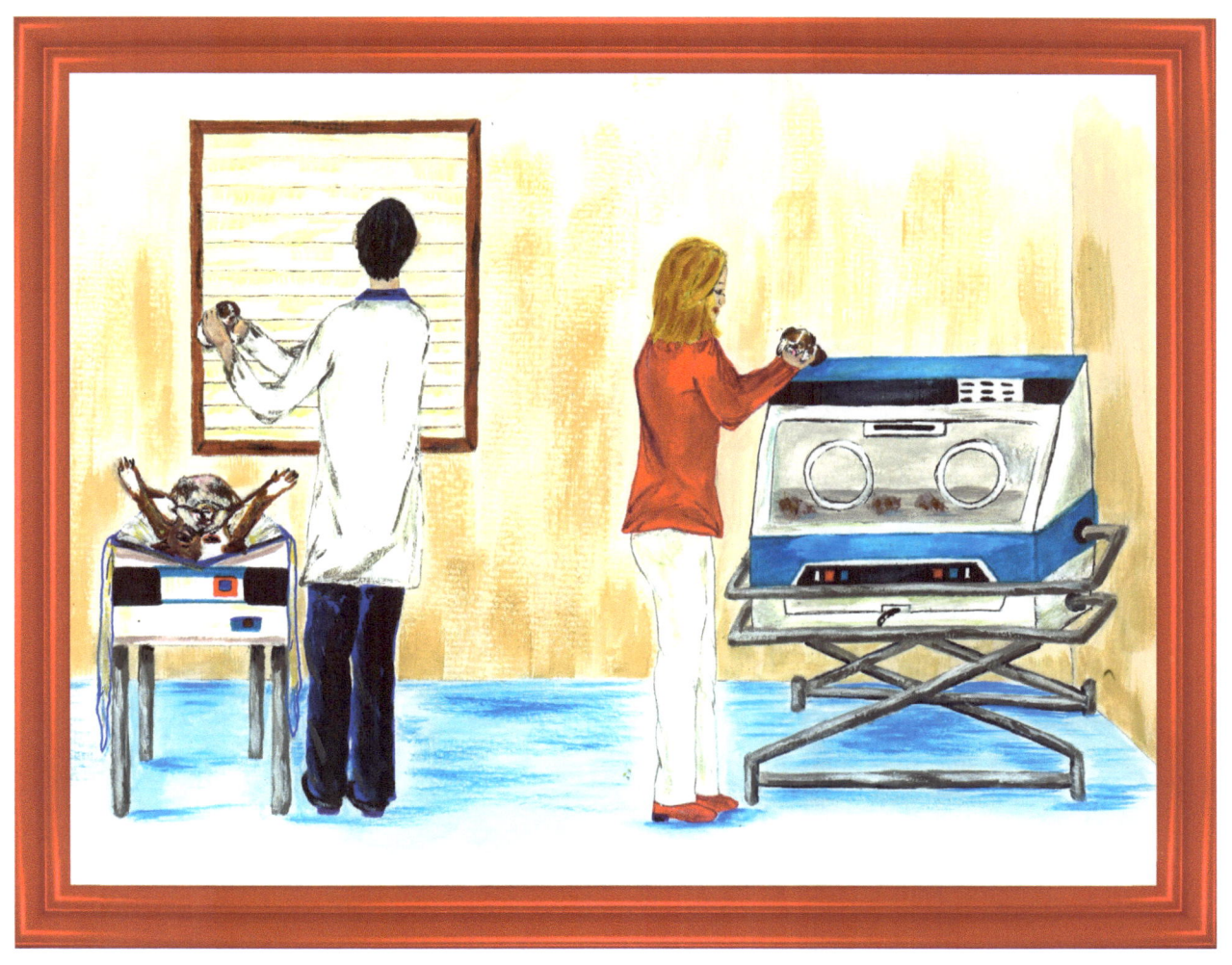

    I know she believed God for a double portion; but, I don't think she expected nine. I knew it would be a big job for the both of us to raise nine bulldog puppies!

We didn't want to lose any of you. Your feedings were every four hours and Mom would have to make sure we didn't sleep through the feedings. Mom saw to it that all of you would get equal feeding time.

She made sure that you stayed warm and clean. When Mom was helping with the feeding, she would talk about how nine puppies made her think of the nine fruits of the spirit described in the Bible. She said they are all produced out of love. Mom read it to me from *Galatians 5:22-23 But the fruit of the spirit is love, joy, peace, longsuffering, gentleness, goodness, faith, meekness, temperance: against such there is no law.*

Six days after you were born, my Dad had to go to the hospital. Days passed and it looked like he would be there a long time. Mom would go to the hospital to be with Dad; and then, she would have to rush home to help with the feeding. This went on for several days. Diego's Mom, Jackie, offered to take care of us so Mom could be with Dad.

I was thrilled! Mom needed the help and I would get to see my true love, Diego, again. We enjoyed the time we spent with them and Jackie taught me how to be a good mother. Finally, time came to say goodbye to Chuck, Jackie, and Diego.

Just as we had to say goodbye to them, tomorrow I will have to say goodbye to you. You will start on your new journey; but, I want you to always remember the love you have in your family.

Never forget the importance of having a good Mother and Father. Having good parents will help equip *you* to be a good parent.

You were produced out of love, just as the fruits of the Spirit are produced out of love. I have named you after the fruits of the Spirit because you have a special gift from God.

Each of you will be going to your own human family. Your purpose in life is to produce your special gift to your new family.

I want to explain why I gave you *special* names.

Destiny, you are named after *Love* because you can give love in the times of the greatest hurts.

Josh, you are full of *Joy* and will bring happiness in the saddest times.

Roni, you will teach *long-suffering* to overcome the hardships of life.

Jeff, you are the peacemaker and will manifest *Peace*.

Stephen, your mild manner displays the spirit of Gentleness.

Darius, you will exhibit *Goodness* when evil abounds.

Nick, Faith has always been your virtue. When all looks hopeless, you will teach your family how to walk in faith.

Caleb, you have endured injury with patience and without resentment. You display *Meekness.*

Chris, you walk each day in *Temperance.* Restraint or self-control is not an easy spirit to produce. You will have the hardest task of all.

Now it is time to go to bed. Sleep well. Tomorrow is a new day for you all!

As the sun rose the next morning, all of the puppies scurried around to get ready for their new journey.

Quickly, come give me one last hug! I hear Mom coming to get you to meet your new family. Mom will make sure we stay in touch. I will be excited to hear how you are blessing your new family.

Will the author be writing a series of books about the adventures of the bulldogs as they go through their journey of life manifesting the fruits of the Spirit? We certainly hope so!

About The Author

Connie Weatherford lost her husband of almost 38 years after a long illness. Ronnie passed January 28, 2011. She thought about giving up the idea of writing this book, but his words of encouragement continued to ring in her ears. This is a true story of her life with Ronnie and is paralleled through the story of her puppies. She raises English Bulldogs and calls them her 'kids.'

Connie's greatest desire is that this book will teach children the true love of God through the fruits of the Spirit, the love of a family, and the obedience to God and parents.

Ronnie had a true love for God and his greatest desire was for his children to serve the Lord.

Connie, Ronnie, (left) Dottie and Rosie, Dottie's pup from another litter.

Acknowledgements

I want to say a special 'Thank You' to my sister and brother-in-law, John and Gwen Titsworth. Gwen has been my spiritual tutor in God and my editor for this book. John has been a great spiritual influence in the life of my family.

I want to thank Jackie and Chuck Evans for taking care of my puppies so I could be at the hospital with Ronnie.

I want to thank Dr. Phil Chitwood, Dr. White and their staff for giving Dottie and her pups such outstanding care and a successful start of nurturing 9 healthy pups. Dr. Phil played a big part in Dottie's special 'mother' experience.

I want to thank Cindy Barr for listening to the voice of the Lord and being willing to go on this venture with us. This is her first time to co-illustrate a children's book.

DOTTIE & DIEGO

Color Us Your Way